2.25

DATE DUE

FEB 16 2001	
APR 2 9 2001	
DEC 3 0 2003	
APR 0 3 2004	
OCT 1 2 2004	
MAR 1 5 2006	

SECRET LIVES OF SNAKES

Eye to Eye with Snakes

Lynn M. Stone

Th ... y, Inc.
...064

PHOTO CREDITS
© J.H. Pete Carmichael: title page, p.9, 16, 18, 21;
© Joe McDonald: p.11, 12, 14; © Lynn M. Stone: cover,
p.4, 6, 13

EDITORIAL SERVICES
Penworthy Learning Systems

Library of Congress Cataloging-in-Publication Data

Stone, Lynn M.
    Secret lives of snakes / Lynn M. Stone.
        p. cm. — (Eye to eye with snakes)
    Summary: Describes how snakes move, reproduce, and hunt for
food.
        ISBN 1-55916-262-7
        1. Snakes—Behavior—Juvenile literature. [1. Snakes—Habits and
behavior.] I. Title.

QL666.06 S8756 2000
597.96'15—dc21   00-025032

1-55916-262-7

Printed in the USA

CONTENTS

THE SNAKE'S LIFE

It is not unusual to find a snake just resting. Snakes may go for hours or days without moving.

Snakes lie in the rays of the sun to warm up. They crawl into shade or into burrows to cool down. Temperatures too hot or too cold tend to make snakes inactive.

Snakes don't spend all their lives, of course, at rest. They must crawl or swim about to hunt for food and to seek mates.

On land, snakes aren't fast, and they have poor eyesight. They remain in a fairly small area all their lives.

Where a snake lives, whether active or at rest, depends upon the **species**, or kind, of snake.

Most kinds of snakes live on land. They can often be found among rocks, leaves, or plants. Some snakes live in and around old farm buildings or dumps. Many snakes live wherever they can find rodents, like rats and mice.

Aquatic and partly aquatic snakes live at least part of their lives in water.

Fox snakes are members of the North American rat snake family. They eat rodents, not foxes, but sometimes give off a foxlike smell.

HOW SNAKES MOVE

When snakes are active, most species move about by crawling on their bellies. Snakes crawl by flexing their muscles from head to tail. The loops, or coils, of their bodies push off against the ground or bark.

A few species move along in unusual ways. The sidewinder rattlesnake, for example, lifts most of its body and flops it forward. This snake uses its head and tail to support the sideways movements of its body.

The top speed of the common garter and rat snakes is about one mile (1.6 m) per hour. You walk much faster than that.

Sidewinder rattlesnakes move with unusual sideways motions. They are found in American deserts near rodent burrows.

The fastest snake may be the African black mamba. For a short time, the long, slender mamba can travel at seven miles (11 km) per hour.

Some aquatic snakes never leave the sea. They travel by swimming or floating. Other snakes, like the American cottonmouths and water snakes, can swim and crawl.

In colder places, snakes cannot be active all year. Each fall they seek shelter in caves or burrows. There the snakes enter a long, sleeplike state called **hibernation**. In spring they awaken.

Snakes are difficult to time, but the black mamba may well be the fastest of snakes. It is also one of the most deadly, a type of cobra without a hood.

This hog-nosed snake of northeastern North America is
perfectly healthy. But to fool predators, it pretends to be
dead. Hog-nosed snakes also hiss and spread their
head and neck cobralike.

The venomous Gaboon viper of Africa is one of the world's deadliest snakes. But it often lies unseen with near-perfect camouflage.

SNAKE BABIES

About four of every five species of snakes lay soft-shelled eggs. The other species bear their young alive.

The number of eggs or live young a snake bears depends upon the species. One species may lay six eggs while another lays over 100. Some snakes have up to 100 live babies!

Snakes usually lay their eggs in rotted logs or shallow holes. Most female snakes lay their eggs and quickly leave them. The eggs of most species hatch in 8 to 10 weeks.

A North American black rat snake coils around her set of eggs, called a clutch.

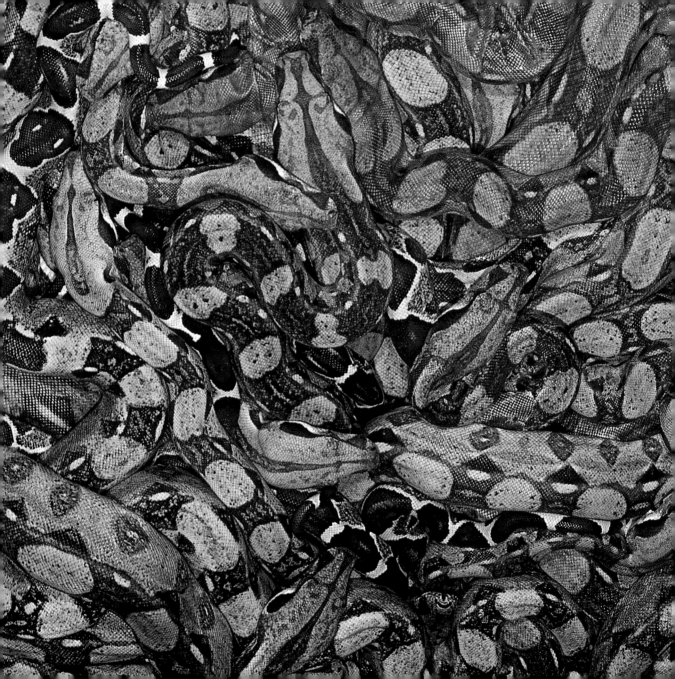

The large python species are unusual. The female python coils around her eggs to **incubate**, or warm, them.

The king cobra is the only snake that scoops a shallow nest for its eggs. The female king cobra then lies in another nest, above her eggs, to guard them.

Baby snakes have no help from their parents. They must catch their own **prey**, or food, and protect themselves.

Only about one kind of snake in five bears its young, like these baby South American boa constrictors, alive.

PREDATOR AND PREY

Most snake species, large and small, catch live prey. Generally snakes eat small mammals, birds, fish, lizards, frogs, toads, or other snakes. A few snakes eat fish eggs, termites, or eggs.

A hunting snake is a **predator**. It feeds on other animals. But sometimes the snake itself becomes prey for stronger, swifter predators. These can include hawks, owls, alligators, or larger snakes.

Snakes usually avoid being prey because their colors often blend into their surroundings. This is called **camouflage**.

From the moment it hatches, this Florida kingsnake will have to take care of itself.

Snakes have other ways to protect themselves, too. A few, like the American hog-nosed snakes, pretend to be dead. Predators aren't as interested in "dead" snakes as live ones.

King snakes and rat snakes rap their tails on leaves when threatened. Scientists believe these **nonvenomous** snakes are trying to sound like **venomous** rattlesnakes.

Frightened water snakes, among others, release a smelly liquid to scare off predators.

Snakes are rarely **aggressive** toward people. They prefer to retreat if given a chance.

This ribbon snake has become the prey of a young sandhill crane on a Florida prairie.

GLOSSARY

aggressive (uh GREH siv) – pushy, forceful

aquatic (uh KWAHT ik) – of water; water loving

camouflage (KAM uh flahj) – the ability to hide by having colors and/or a shape that blends in with the surroundings

hibernation (hi ber NAY shun) – a deep, sleeplike state into which certain animals go each winter

incubate (ING kyoo bayt) – to keep warm, especially the warming of eggs

nonvenomous (NAHN ven uh mus) – refers to a snake that does not produce venom, a poison

predator (PRED uh ter) –a animal that hunts and kills other animals for food

prey (PRAY) – an animal that is hunted for food by another animal

species (SPEE sheez) – within a group of closely related animals, such as rattlesnakes, one certain type (*black-tailed* rattlesnake)

venomous (VEN uh mus) – refers to a snake that produces venom, a poison

FURTHER READING

Find out more about snakes with these helpful books:

Greer, Dr. Allen. **Reptiles**, Time Life, 1996

McCarthy, Colin. **Reptile**. Alfred Knopf, 1991

Schnieper, Claudia. **Snakes, Silent Hunters**. Carolrhoda, 1995

Simon, Seymor. **Snakes**. Harper Collins, 1994

INDEX